GIVE
LIFE
A
CHANCE

RESTORATIVE JUSTICE

ROBERT B STANLEY

Give Life a Chance
Copyright © 2022 by Robert B Stanley

All rights reserved. No part of this publication may be reproduced, distributed, or transmitted in any form or by any means, including photocopying, recording, or other electronic or mechanical methods, without the prior written permission of the author, except in the case of brief quotations embodied in critical reviews and certain other non-commercial uses permitted by copyright law.

tellwell

Tellwell Talent
www.tellwell.ca

ISBN
978-0-2288-7957-2 (Hardcover)
978-0-2288-7956-5 (Paperback)
978-0-2288-7958-9 (eBook)

TABLE OF CONTENTS

Foreword v
When Tomorrow Starts Without Me vii

Chapter 1 The Day That Changed a Families Life Forever ... 1

    The Act 3
    Finding out 8
    Frustration 16

Chapter 2 Case Development 21

    Alberta Conflict Transformation Society 30
    Court outcome 32

Chapter 3 The Letter of Apology 35

    To the Stanley family 36
    The Family 37
    The Conference 40
    The Stanley Family Makes The Right Choice 49
    Turning Point 51

Chapter 4 Restorative Justice Direction 55

    Forgive and forget 60
    Give Life a Chance 61
    Robert Bruce Stanley Bio 64

In Loving Memory of

Bob Stanley
1926 - 2002

FOREWORD

This book is written in memory of my father - Robert Arthur Stanley, also to the Restorative Justice Community which before the murder of our father we had no knowledge or the organization.

Restorative Justice has been around for a few years prior to my fathers' murder and the first high profile criminal case in Canada. With the arrest of and court appearance(s) of the person(s) who were responsible and eventually charged in the murder the Judge in the case along with the Prosecutor and the Defense lawyer asked for the Organization (ACTS) (Alberta Conflict Transformation Society) and the teen accused in the murder wanted to arrange a meeting with the family and one of the persons that committed the murder.

Alberta Conflict Transformation Society and Restorative Justice Society encompasses five elements in the conference meeting. These elements consist in the meeting – narrative – the emotional understanding of the process and agreement between the two parties, the person(s) harmed and the person(s) who committed the harm. In the conference there are principals which is in focus:

1. Repair – crime causes harm and justice requires repairing that harm.
2. Encounter - the best way to determine how to do this to have the parties decide together.

My story of this process and how it runs through the elements of the process. It starts with my family history through to the murder of our father and the heart ache we went through for four long years before there was a person(s) arrested and brought to justice that committed the murder.

Parts of the book will be descriptive on how the murder was devised at the start through time and how time changes a person. Dates of the process of when the person(s) involved went through the thoughts to commit the actions in the murder through to the court proceedings as best told to the family and the detectives investigating. The proceeding that took place in a timeline and the emotions of getting even in a harsh attitude with the person(s) who committed the murder. As the case proceeded through the timeline to the meeting of the persons harmed and the person(s) that committed the harm to the changes of minds of the family as the book title describes. **GIVE LIFE A CHANCE** and how I chose the title.

WHEN TOMORROW STARTS WITHOUT ME

When tomorrow starts without me, I am not there to see.
If the sun should rise and find your
eyes all filled with tears for me.
I wish so much you would not cry the way you did today,
While thinking of the many things we did not get to say.
I know how much you love me, as much as I love you,
And each time you think of me, I
know you will miss me too,
And that id must leave behind all the thing dear to me hear
But when tomorrow starts without
me, please try to understand,
That an angel came and called my name
and took me by the hand,
And said my place is ready now in heaven far above, and
that I would have to leave behind all those I dearly love.
But as I turn to walk away, a tear fell from my eye,
For all my life, I had always thought I did one want to die.
It seems almost impossible that I am leaving you.
But the road to love will end in grief no mater what we do.
I thought of all the yesterdays, the good one's and the bad,
I thought of all the love we shared and all the fun we had.
If I could relive yesterday, I thought, just for a while,
I would say good-bye and kiss you and see you smile.
But when I fully realised that this could never
be, but when I walked through Heaven
the emptiness and memories would take the place of me.

And when I thought of worldly things
that I would miss tomorrow,
I thought of you, and when I did, my
heart was filled with sorrow.
But when turned I walked through Heaven's
gate, I felt so much at home.
When God looked down and smiled at
me, from the great golden throne,
He said, "this is eternity, and all I promised you.
Today your life on earth has passed, but here it starts anew.
I promise not tomorrow, but today will always last,
And since each days the same day,
there is no looking for the past.
You will see that I was faithful, forgiving, and so true.
Tough there were times you did some
things you know you should not do.
But you have been forgiven, and now at last your free.
So, wont you take my hand and share my life with me?"
So, when tomorrow starts without me
Do not think were far apart, for every time you
think of me, I am right here in your heart.

(Unknown Author)

CHAPTER

1

THE DAY THAT CHANGED A FAMILIES LIFE FOREVER

BRUCE EDWARDS, THE JOURNAL, FILE

The teen used wire cutters to make a hole in the mesh fence of the pedestrian overpass near 113th Street to push the boulder onto Stanley's bus.

THE ACT

My family consist of, my Father Robert Stanley, Mother Audrey, brothers Byron, Rick, Wayne, and myself Bruce.

Our lives even after we married and had children of our own, always evolved our lives around one another. Taking family vacations from the earlier days in France on the Riviera up to recent vacations in the Rock Mountains in Canada.

We celebrated Christmases and Birthdays together and enjoyed gatherings in the back yards, for any occasions. Memories like these of our lives together, brought us together as a happy and a loving family group even up to the present. We always shared and appreciated each other company.

Dad, the main figure in all our lives was a harsh person in his ways but fare in his actions. As said, many times he was a gentle giant from the oiled school where at times he kept saying "I use to walk 5 miles to school and back, we never had the luxury of transportation". He was a role model in our lives, a kind of individual that cared for life cared and for others that were involve in the life of Robert Stanley. He was a man who was liked by everyone he encountered whether in play or at work.

Always competitive with his love of sports, especially hockey. Dad played hockey while in the Canadian Armed Forces and played quit well and if you can imagine him just as a great hockey player (Gordy Howe), he was a particularly good in his younger years. Just as good and dirty but fare as Howe was. With that in mind it flowed into other sports later in his years. Dad loved and shined in competition as his love in curling and shuffleboard. Dad and I played shuffleboard, and I would complete together in the local leagues.

His career over a span of 30 years was in the Royal Canadian Air Force. With our father in the Air Force, we as a family myself and Byron lived throughout his posting throughout Canada and in Europe. In the Canadian Air Force Air Movements as air crew, he flew around the world in many types of aircraft. In his work it carried him as air crew cargo head to passenger to official crew to Queen Elizabeth a few times.

Over the last years after Dad's murder, remembering Dad and an amazing life we had together, the good and tough times but the enjoyable time in our lives we had as a close nit family, as if it were yesterday. All those memories came **crashing** down, taking casualties Dads brothers and sister, my brothers and myself and our families the many dozens of his friends right to the children he loved on his school bus job. Each of us have our own memories, **crashed to a halt**. A day of a senseless act that will live in the memories of the Stanley family, forever in our hearts and all our minds. An experience I recall like it was yesterday that happened on a clear Saturday morning in June. As we continually think about and recall the events that unfolded up to the murder of our father.

It was early Saturday morning June 1, 2002, our father (Robert Stanley) doing what he loved to do in his retirement was driving his school bus and after his regular work do extra charter trips. On this day Dad had completed the charter that evening and on his way to the central office to park for the night. He travelled west bound on the Whitemud Freeway in the far-left lane.

As a school bus driver, the children well liked him he drove to and from school on his steady route. He would often joke around with the kids supplying the young riders with treats while chatting with them on their daily travels. The way he treated them and call the children on his bus as his children, always making sure they were always safe, demonstrated how he treated all the people he got to know throughout his life.

It was just after midnight – dad was on his way home, first to return the bus to the shop, then drive home and eventually meet up with me for our shuffleboard games that morning. He was traveling in the outside closest to the center medium, unknown to dad who was very fit, and sound minded individual for his age of seventy-five, met a group of teenagers out celebrating their grade nine graduation. The teenagers for unknown reasons at the time had chosen to do a dangerous foolish and completely senseless act by tossing a large bolder off the foot bridge overpass.

The teens after gathering at one of the teenagers' homes where a group of up to five consumed alcohol and used drugs. Peer pressure was also known was determined as a factor. The idea to get a big rock, cut holes in the overpass screen (which was cut out before hand) at the home of one of the teenagers and thought and wanted do damage a large vehicle that would pass under the overpass.

Again, Dad was doing extra work after hours and he was doing what he loved. Driving a school bus in his retirement. After finishing his extra work, head back to the shop late on Friday night. Early Saturday morning June 1, 2002, morning as dad traveled west bound underneath the pedestrian overpass, located about 106 St and the Whitemud Freeway which is located just south of the Southgate Shopping Centre.

Above him while traveling under the overpass, not seen by dad, two of the 15-year-old teenagers that earlier cut three holes in the fencing over each lane of west bound traveling lanes set up by carrying a large basketball sized boulder from a near by garden in the area. In a moment of stupidity, senseless and irresponsible placed the boulder on the railing at one of the holes cut out by the teens (the teenagers acquired a pair of wire cutters from their house) with the boulder set on the railing over the lane dad was traveling.

The teens plan was to wait for a large vehicle (we learned later) to toss the boulder through hole cut out over the railing edge. It was then that Dads bus approached and in an instant that boulder met the upper front medal frame of the of the driver's side windshield, pushing the metal inwards and smashing through the upper part of the windshield. Dad never saw the boulder coming down onto him, it smashed through the windshield crashing into dad's chest crushing his chest. The force generated by the weight of the boulder (30kg), the distance and speed of the boulder dropping, and the speed of dads' bus was great enough to do (did) major damage and major injury (the force killed dad almost instant. We were told dad death was almost instant. He was found out of the seat on the floor where he only had time phone in hand dialed only the first three numbers of his home number before passed away to his major injury.

How the bus was found I can only imagine by the grace of God and his training and experience, how he managed to pull the bus off the travel portion of the roadway, onto the side next to the meridian wall and put his four ways (hazard lights) on.

There were witnesses at the time of the incident which asked they said the bus brake (seeing the brake lights) pulled over in control and the 4-way hazard light activated. Seemed the everything was ok, interrupted as if the there was mechanical problems, and all was good. Over the span of two hours, a police patrol passed by, not noticing anything out of the ordinary until they return east bound when they noticed something was not right by looking at the windshield. They turned around and came back to check on the bus stopped on the side of the road. At that time, the police found dad inside the bus on the floor and discovered his major injuries.

One of the members called for an ambulance while the other perform life saving response first aid and when the ambulance arrived and the tried to revive dad and transported him to the hospital where he was pronounced deceased.

FINDING OUT

That morning I had taken my wife (Diane) to work, returning home I got some breakfast and as I eat, I stood by the front door looking outside waiting for dad to come by and pick me up. At the same time, I had the tv on and listening to morning news. The broadcaster come on and said that there was a bus driver injured while driving the bus on the Whitemud freeway last night. I turned to look at the tv and saw in the broadcast a bus parked on the left side of the freeway next to the meridian wall with 4-way hazard lights on. The picture of the bus was a shot from a long distance and appeared it was parked there maybe because of mechanical problems. The broadcaster saying there was no information the condition of the driver or why he was injured. It was said the bus was found shortly after midnight June 1, 2002. It did not dawn on me that the driver was my father as there are always school buses on charter work on the weekends.

Every Saturday morning Dad picked me up and we would go to the Army, Navy, Air Force Club to play Shuffleboard. He usually came by about 8.30 then we travelled together to the club. However, as I waited and watched the news, I received a phone call. It was from the Edmonton Police Service and identifying himself as a detective telling me that my father had been seriously injured earlier that morning. In shock with what the detective said to be my mind and gaze went to the bus I saw on the news. Still, I had no idea as to the seriousness of the situation and that it even was to do with my father.

On receiving the scary phone call from the police detective, he said that I should go to Dad's house, there he would meet me. Not finished with the police, I question him to how serious it was, I had trouble believing him at that point. I was in the dark as why the police called. The detective just said that the information I was asking of him, the question and answer was not for over the phone and to please come to the house.

I did say to the detective I had to go and pick up my wife from work and would hurry to the house. The detective yes please pick up your wife and come straight to the house. I was in shock not getting answers from the police but hung up and called my wife. I called Diane at work and said to her the police just called asked for me to go to Dad's place and there the police would answer any question I had. She said what is going on. I said to her, I do not know all I was told to get you and come to the house. As we know that a lot of thoughts go through a person mind, but I was not prepared for what was going to be told to me when I got to the house. When I arrived at the house, I saw my brothers' vehicles also there and Diane was asked to go straight into the house, but the detective stopped me before I had a chance to go in.

He held me there for a few minutes. He stood in front of me where he told me what happened to my father, he was seriously injured. At that point I reflected to earlier this morning to what I saw on the news. I asked him, did it have to do with what I saw on the news this morning. The detective then put his hand on my shoulder and told me the driver was my father and he had passed away from his injuries.

What seemed an exceptionally long time, I started crying saying "no it can't be, it not true." The detective with his hand on my shoulder, he was sorry to have to tell me the of my father's death but said he had questions he had to ask. At that point I said am I a suspect to my own father death. He did say, no that it is just a formality. He asked where I was that morning? "I said at home." Where was I all night? "I said at home." Was I at home at the time of the incident? "I said yes." I did say "again I asked, are you saying I am suspected in what happened to father"? The detective said no, I must ask questions like this.

When I got into dads' home there was the family (dads' wife) (Rick, Wayne, Diane, Ziane, Emily, Hollie, Bobbie, Curtis, and myself). Byron, my brother arrived from Jasper a little later. While we were gathered in the house, it was then the detectives on the investigation explained the details that dad had been driving west bound on the Whitemud freeway where a large boulder was drop from the pedestrian overpass on the freeway onto Dad's bus. The large boulder went through the windshield striking him in the chest which caused the death of our father.

After the family was told how Dad was killed and hearing the horrible way it happed, all in disbelief, angry, and frustrated, all asked did the detective know who did this and why someone would think of doing this. In turn the detectives asked if there was anyone that we could think of that could be held responsible in our fathers' murder. We said that Dad did not have any enemies, he was well liked and had many friends. That morning all our lives came crashing down, each and everyone of us. The detectives said they would keep us informed as things came up. Also, there would be another detective group from the Edmonton Police would be in contact with the family later.

We were all angry and we let the detectives here this anger through our voices. If we get our hands on the person or persons responsible for the murder, we will do the same to that person or persons. The detectives heard the anger and talked some of the family members down saying that this would not help the case and to let the justice system do its job. Yes, they could feel the anger in the voices but asked not to think in such a way as that. They said let us get the person or persons responsible and the system will do the rest.

Yes, there were members of the family wanting to get their hands on the person and do an eye for an eye. But the police pleaded not to think that way. They said when the person(s) is caught we would have our days in court. The family after some time with the police settled down and asked to make sure all developments in Dad's murder passed to the family. They assured us they would.

GREG SOUTHAM, THE JOURNAL
The media take photos on Tuesday of the rock that killed Robert Stanley.

BRUCE EDWARDS, THE JOURNAL, FILE
The teen used wire cutters to make a hole in the mesh fence of the pedestrian overpass near 113th Street to push the boulder onto Stanley's bus.

Stanley managed to get his bus off to the shoulder of Whitemud Drive after a boulder, tossed from the pedestrian bridge in the background, crashed through his windshield on the night of May 31, 2002.

...ield of school bus driver Robert Stanley.

– Supplied photos

n the
rock
was

nley's
(top)
deadly
photos
court.

18

FRUSTRATION

The person(s) that committed the murder of our father had not come forward or had been identified for more than 3 years. Frustration, anger, and the talk of revenge was talked about between the family and was also said when we met with the detectives. This action and words are common when a family and a loved one is taken away suddenly especially murdered. Where the frustration was coming from was that it was taking a long time for the detectives to answer our questions (why this happened, who is the responsible persons), three long agonizing years with nothing. We, as a family said to the police that the feeling of suspicion, they were not telling us everything. The main detective Ernie Schreiber was consistently visiting the family at my place giving updates. The same message repeatedly was all he could say. We asked if you know something please tell us. We need answers, positive answers a shrug of the shoulders and comment nothing has changed.

Eventually the detective Ernie Schreiber came to the family at my home informing us that they had a person of interest in Dad's case. We all looked at each other saying, its about time! We asked - Who is this person? Can we see him? Ernie also gave us more information in the case but still not revealing everything as Ernie said, "there is evidence they have protected, and the person(s) can only fill the details." Throughout the 3 years he said there was a lot of information, and they had many leads but held off until now, as the case opened. The family started to believe that the case would turn cold, and the murderer would never be caught. The actions in the case, as we found out, in the police investigation they were watching persons of interest. The police went as far as putting a police female undercover to get information from the group they were watching. We were shocked to learn the female detective could pass as a teenager. He also said, anything more on Dad's case he promised to keep us update as more positive information became known. With the information passed to us gave hope the case was still being investigated.

During this time, the police had a person of interest and not yet charged. Detective Ernie Schreiber contact the family about this person and asked to meet with the family at my house. The family got together and met at my home where Ernie filled us in on more information he received in the case. During this meeting, Ernie described the situation on how he fit the profile in the evidence the had. The person of interest they were holding had said he was the one that did the murder our father, but they needed more solid proof.

Ernie then asked if one members of the family would want to come to the station and meet this person face to face. We took some time and talked as a family and decided that I would go to the meeting. On arrival at the police station, Detective Ernie Schreiber met me along with two other detectives on the dads' case, Cal Kowton and Darren Hodson who had also came to the house with support and information. I learned that all the actions by the detectives was part of the duties of the police to gather information and fill in the holes they were keeping from the public and the family. It was all part of the investigation to weed out people and end with the correct individual that is responsible for the murder.

They met me at the front of the police station where they talked to me how I was to manage the interview. I was taken to a room where they had me stand against a wall with Ernie and Darren standing on both sides of me. There was a table in the center of the room with two chairs on both sides of the table. Once I was standing at the wall, Cal and a police officer brought the person of interest into the room, they had walked by me, on my left side about six feet away and had him stand against the wall on the other side of the room with the table between us. There Cal and another police officer stood on either side of this male person. As he walks by me my stomach started to twist and all I could do was just stand there shacking all over and staring. I found out later after the interview, the detectives positioned all four of us that way they were for my protection and encase the anger overwelled me and they could prevent me from attacking this person.

I did not say much but asked "why did you murder my father? Do you know the man (father) you murdered? Are you that insensitive? Why did you wait this long to come forward? I do not understand why you would do such a mindless act. There really was no response from this person standing across from me, I was getting sick to my stomach just listening to this murderer. I could not stay in this meeting any longer and I asked to leave and after in the hallway apologized to Ernie. He said I did fine. There is no right way stand in front of a person that murdered your father. That was the really the hardest thing I have ever done in my life, was to stand in front of a person, with tears in my eyes, who murdered my father.

After the meeting at the police station with this suspect I stood in front of, he was released. Wow! now the family struck a new level madness, frustration, anger, and disbelief in the solving of our father's murder. The detectives said, they have no clue and dads murder will never be found. Ernie met with us and understood the position we were all in, and his team was in the same space, but he did explain the process he was going through and let us know there was a group they have been watching. He also said that the person I saw turned himself in and this person is the type that does this for attention. Ernie said, besides this person had no details on how the murder was committed, he was clueless and could not fill the holes. He did say that with details in the case hidden from the media and the family, the person(s) that committed the murder would and could fill them in. Ernie said that the details held back from us was so the way the media asks questions, a person could slip and use words that the media could pick up on, as well as they are trained, (they did trust us) could get the information and publish it and make the person(s) they are looking for stay hiding and never come forward.

During the years, the three detectives were steadily consulting the family, doing it on a regular basis. The objective was to keep our hopes up in the family and as you can understand there was scepticism for the family members were losing hope and faith the case in dad's murder. Throughout the years we felt that the detectives were not telling us all the facts and the evidence was not on our side. One thing is that the boulder was not worked on for evidence because the crimes lab, who is the RCMP forensic lab was to busy for our case.

Too busy did not sitting well with the family. The lab was working a case out of BC. It was the Pickton case, and the pig farm murders. Then we were told the boulder had been shipped to the United States for the forensic work, to top it off Ernie informed us that the evidence such as DNA was not there or through shipping it had been lost because of the handling too many times. **FRUSTRATION** set in again. It seemed as if the murder of our father would go unsolved.

"THAT MOMENT IN TIME, OUR LIVES, OUR MINDS AND FAITH IN THE SOLVING THE MURDER WAS SLOWLY DISAPPEARING"

Anger being upset and unimaginable words in our thoughts. All crying out and asking **(how and who could do such a senseless act and not feel guilty and not come forward with all that guilt).**

CHAPTER II
CASE DEVELOPMENT

Bruce Stanley, left, and his brothers Wayne and Byron, right, the sons of Robert Stanley, speak to the media following the sentencing hearing of a teen who threw a boulder from a Whitemud Drive overpass. The boulder killed Stanley when it smashed through his windshield.

JUNE 1, 2002

Robert Stanley murdered while driving the school bus on the Whitemud Freeway

AUGUST 17, 2005

- Edmonton police announced that a youth had been charged with manslaughter of Robert Stanley. Due to the age of the person, under the Youth Criminal Justice Act The name of the offender can not be identified.
- The police spokesperson said the suspect had been on the radar for some time. From early in the investigation this person was of interest as far as the investigation was concerned
- The police had dealt with this person in terms of interviews early in the investigation and needed to pay more attention to him.
- Police detective working the case said the killing was not premeditated through this the investigators claimed it was a prank gone wrong.
- Because of the family's attitude and wanting the harshest sentence the Detectives explained the differences between - first degree - second degree - third degree and manslaughter and if we went the wrong way the teen could end up not guilt and walk away. Therefore first, second and third degree would not hold so the only charge that would be laid is manslaughter.

- The investigator said "what I am telling you, this is the person we are holding responsible for manslaughter, with the conviction carrying a maximum life term in prison. But the Defense and the Crown can also apply for a youth sentence for manslaughter, which would be a maximum three years.
- The teen did not enter a plea and was set to appear in court again on September 7, 2005. He was release from custody on bail after he was charged. He was initially placed on house arrest, but the condition was varied so he could keep his job as a laborer.

OCTOBER 12, 2005 *(CHARGES STAYED)*

- Alberta Justice announced the Crown had stayed the manslaughter charges against the young offender charged to dad's murder. Because unforeseeable and unexpected evidence had come forward making the likelihood of a conviction unreasonable and the charges were dropped and let go.
- This was the person I met in person at the police station.
- We were told, because the accused was a youth not being the right individual and the information that came forward, he could not fill the proper answers and not giving the details, the police were looking for that is why the charges were stayed. This gave the investigator more time (1 year) and the momentum in the case.

- Staying the case gives the police a window of one year to re-activate the case. since the youth was charged the investigation continued before and after.
- The families' current thoughts with the development of the case and the many questions, if there would ever be a person caught in the murder.
- Police announced the arrest of two of the teens after additional information came forward after the first youth was arrested. Investigators said they arrested the youth who throw the rock as well as the youth who helped carry the rock to the bridge.
- The young offender prior to this date was tormented with guilt in the killing of my father Robert Stanley that he along with his father went to the police station and turned himself in.
- My fathers murder case took four long years to get to this stage. As far as the family was concerned and believed that the murder of our father would never be solved, and we could not get closure and really find out who the person(s) was that committed the murder and ask questions on how and why and why this senseless act was done.
- What happened on the footbridge on June 1, 2002, had remained a secret kept by five teenagers? Their silence ended when someone outside the group was charged with manslaughter.
- News of the arrest of the 19-year-old in August caused the unidentified women to come forward, telling the police that she and for others were on the bridge at the time of the incident. Interviews were

conducted with all five person and the police were able to determine which two were responsible.
- The original suspect who was fifteen at the time of the incident, have been charged with one count of manslaughter. These teens can not be identified publicly under the Youth Criminal Justice Act.
- On November 16, 2002, two teens in the case made their first appearance in youth court and we each prosecuted on a charge of Manslaughter.

MARCH 17, 2006 (ONE TEEN PLEADS GUILTY)

- One of the two teens pleaded guilt to manslaughter. He was ordered to undergo a psychiatric assessment before his sentence date.
- With no criminal record the teens lawyer is asking for a non-custodial sentence. However, the prosecutor would and did recommend jail time.
- That evening on May 31, 2002, there was a grade nine graduation ceremony at the Catholic Junior High School. There were a group of teens along with the two accused in the murder split a bottle of liquor at one of their homes.
- That day the teen who pleaded guilt along with four others planned to drop something off the nearby footbridge onto a large vehicle such as transport truck or a bus.
- The group went looking for a larger boulder in the area close to the footbridge and found a garden round boulder about a block away weighing about 30

kg. the two accused along with three friends lugged the boulder to the east side of the footbridge near 113 Street
- The fifteen-year-old teens at the time grabbed a pair of wire cutters from the house and cut three holes in the steel grading wire over each lane on the west bound lanes (north side of the footbridge) close to 113 street.
- When the holes were cut the two accused pickup the boulder once the saw a larger vehicle approaching (it was a bus, my father's bus) in the far-left lane they then they pushed and dropped it onto the bus.
- After the teens dropped the boulder onto dad's school bus and hearing the boulder crashing onto the bus. The group ran off the footbridge. The teen who was last off the footbridge told the police that as he ran, he looked down at where the bus was and saw the brake lights on the bus and it stop on the freeway on the left side.
- He did not know the driver was hurt until the next day they learned the driver our father (Robert Stanley) had died of his injuries.
- The five teens that were part of the murder met and made a packed to never talk about what had happened that night on the footbridge. That lasted for four exceptionally long and agonizing years until guilt took over. The other three were not charge and the family asked why not. As explained to us is by the detectives, in Canada there is no provision in the courts to charge accomplices in a murder. We also questioned the charge, as the teens planned and

executed the plan was this not premeditated murder and should carry a harsher sentence. The answer "it is up to the courts to determine the act and the sentence could reflect it"

MAY 24, 2006

- The second teen charged foe manslaughter of the murder of our father (Robert Stanley) appeared in court. Unlike the first teen the second pleaded no guilty and elected to proceed to trial. His next court date was set for November 20, 2006
- The family could not believe the actions of the second teen, who under the Youth Criminal Act could not be officially named, and with the evidence the investigation finally had, he pleaded not guilty. We were informed that the action was under the guidance of his lawyer and family.

JUNE 13, 2006

- The teen who pleaded guilty of manslaughter appeared in court for sentencing arguments.

    Crown Prosecution – (David Hill) asked for three-year term in which two years in confinement and one year under supervision.

    Defense Lawyer - (Rick Stroppel) called for no jail time. Suggesting instead house arrest and perform community service.

Stanley Family

- the family sentiment towards the sentencing was different from the what the Crown and Defence asked for. The family did not want the teen to be behind bars. The family believed through a turn and a belief our father would think, there was genuine remorse, and the teen was a straight "A" student, a good-looking kid, he would not survive jail, or he would be turned into a criminal.
- In dad's memory on how our father always thought and raised us boys, which he was fair gave us chances. This teen was a kid that did a stupid prank. He was not a bad kid just caught up with the wrong side of life.

ALBERTA CONFLICT TRANSFORMATION SOCIETY

Through the process, ACTS championed the conference spearheaded by Sue Hopgood with Caroline Gosling and the detectives on the case Ernie Schrieber, Cal Kowton and Darren Hodson with both my family and the first teens family. The process was the meeting in Edmonton on June 4, 2006, for seven hours the Stanley family and the teen that committed the murder and his family met in a conference circle. The conference circle had twenty-five family members from both sides and with the coordinators and the detectives it made for an exceptionally long and hot meeting. The process in Community Conferencing and Restorative Justice is too met get to understand the harm and solve the harm with a mutual agreement.

The teen we met with wanted to have a chance to explain why he delayed in coming forward. As said through the guilt built up inside him that he had to come forward because he did not want to keep the secret any longer. Through the meeting and my experience in life, I have never witnessed a person knock themselves down, degrading themself and calling down on his own stupidity saying he was a coward and was not man enough to come forward.

- Teen one – he felt (real) bad what he had done in making lives a living hell for so long. He kept saying he was sorry" I've cause hell for your family" and yes, he made our lives a living hell with an emptiness in each member of my family. He, "I've mess up so much and I'm so sorry." This is where we all saw true remorse. One thing we all can define remorse but in the true meaning is when you really see it. When looking at the persons eyes the difference is no remorse is black emptiness in the eyes where true remorse is for real is the eyes have color and, in a way, you see inside a person. The other is body action and position.

- Teen two – when the second teen was charged in our fathers' murder, his decision, more than likely made by his lawyer, pleaded not guilty (but the family new he was guilty) and elected to go to trial. The case was heard on November20, 2006. One thing we all can define remorse but in the true meaning is when you really see it. When looking at the persons eyes the difference is no remorse is black emptiness in the eyes where true remorse is for real is the eyes have color and, in a way, you see inside a person. The other is body action and position. The second teen did not show any remorse and his actions were not looking at the family in court with the eyes looking down at the floor and word of discouragement, nothing in the apology, but two words "I'm sorry" disappointing from a youth that participated in the murder of our father.

COURT OUTCOME

On June 22, 2006, the Honourable Judge D. Dalton reserved the decision. The teen will be sentenced as a youth and the name(s) can not be publish because of his age at the time of the offence.

At the time of the offence in 2002 the Youth Criminal Act was enforced and then justice system application changed in 2003 to Youth Criminal Justice Act. Because of the confusion in the two laws and which application would take effect the teen could receive a non jail sentence.

Because of the two laws Judge D. Dalton wanted to review and understand what the is in this case. The Defence lawyer Rick Stroppily stated that because of the change in the law he asked for a non jail sentence.

Judge D. Dalton adjourned the proceedings giving her the time to make the right sentence with the new laws and she gave a one-week time span needed to review even tough the issue was resolved.

JUNE 29, 2006

> On the reconvening of the court, Judge D. Dalton sentenced the teen calling his actions was (adolescent stupidity at its zenith)
>
> Dalton said the so-called prank which led to Stanley's death, "was not a spontaneous act, but a deliberate

premeditated undertaking. The Judge did accept the intent was to do vandalism not to hurt anyone.

It was pointed out to the family; the act was manslaughter however the case could have turned to a lesser conclusion. The act could have changed to a mischief charge, not manslaughter, to a mischief charge with no harm to anyone. It was told to the family that manslaughter shift to mischief charge by estimates the time difference of as little as 1/10 of a second. We thought yes but that does not bring our father back. We lost all that should have been.

The teen at the time of the act his age was fifteen and after four long years his age the time of the court case is nineteen years old. He was sentenced to six months Deferred Custody followed by eighteen months probation. He will service house arrest and will perform 240 hours of community service.

There were mandatory terms given him

- Keep the peace and be of good behaviour
- Appear before the youth justice court when required by the court to do so
- Report to the Provincial Director immediately upon release, and then be under the supervision of the Provincial Director
- Inform the Provincial immediately on being arrested or questioned by the police officer
- Report to the police officer or any named individual, as instructed by the Provincial Director

- Advise the Provincial Director of his address of residence on release and after release report immediately to the Provincial Director of any change.
  - In that address
  - In his normal occupation, including employment, vocational or educational training and volunteer work
  - In his family or financial situation and that may be expected to affect his ability to comply with the conditions of the sentence
  - Not own, posses or have the control of a weapon, ammunition, prohibited ammunition, prohibit device or explosive substance
  - Comply with any reasonable instructions that the Provincial Director considers necessary in respect of any condition of the conditional supervision to prevent a breach of that condition or to protect society

Courts have also instructed the teen to write a public apology to be given to the media and the Stanley family.

CHAPTER III

THE LETTER OF APOLOGY

TO THE STANLEY FAMILY

I am sincerely sorry for the loss and grief that I have caused you. The pain that you have endured I tremendous to loss a loved one in such a manner is awful, I am deeply sorry for all that I have done and put everyone through.

I am so sorry for hiding away all these years and for not coming forward immediately. I was too much of a coward and too scared to face the consequences of what I had done. It was my stupidity and recklessness behaviour that caused this tragedy. I did not know what to at such an early age. This is not an excuse and I now take full responsibility for my actions. So much pain could have been prevented if I would have come forward years ago.

I know that the victim could have been anyone. It could have been one of my family members. If someone else was taken I such a way, I do not know if could ever forgive. I would like to thank all of you for not seeing me as a monster. It will still be a long time before I can truly forgive myself.

Your entire family has demonstrated so much compassion for me. What you have shown me through our conference was life changing. your reaction and input encouraged me to make something of myself. You have given me a second chance; I hope I can give back after I have taken so much.

Deeply remorseful
Signed by the teen

THE FAMILY

My family in its entirety was my Father Robert Stanley – Mother Audrey – my Brothers Byron wife Emily, son Chris, daughter Jody – Rick wife Karen, son Shawn, daughter Salina – Wayne wife Ziane, daughter Amanda, son Ethan and dads present wife Judy.

Our lives, even after we married and had children of our own, had always evolved around one another. Taking family vacations right from the earlier years in Europe and the French Riviera to in later years through the Rocky Mountains.

We will never again be celebrated Christmas, birthdays together as a whole family and enjoying the numerous gatherings in the back yards for all vacations with our father. Our mother Audrey always in our thoughts on special occasions passed away of cancer in October 1986. Memories like ours brought us together as a happy and loving group of individuals who always shared and appreciated each other.

Dad was harsh in his ways but fair in his actions which spread to the brothers. He was a role model, a kind of individual that cared for life and others around him in highest regards. This was a man who was liked by all in play and at work. His friends and friendship spread over time and in all place's dad was.

Always competitive in all he did from games with his family (especially his grandson Curtis) to the love for hockey. Our father, if you could vision him, was a particularly good hockey player in his younger years, I used to compare him with the likes NHL Gordie Howe. In his hockey days he was just as good and clean dirty but as he would say to me, I am always clean and fare on the ice. (Yah, sure dad, you did not take any prisoners on the ice, clean as he used to say). That type of personality spread into his love in shuffleboard where he was just as sharp and competitive even with his grandson and all of us.

Dad and me in his last days played the game together and I can say, I could never take him on and win. His competitiveness was still there and as evident. Even on his son he always ribbed me that he is the winner and laugh. Miss you dad and love you very much as do all of us.

One day 20 years ago, all those memories I have reflected on and remembered came crashing down, taking lots of casualties. A day of a senseless act that will live on forever in the hearts and minds of the Stanley family. This senseless act I recall like it was yesterday that happened on a clear Saturday morning June 1, 2002, while wait for dad at the front door to pick me up for or shuffleboard day.

The hardest memory for us brothers to recall in the week's entirety up to the day our father was murdered. Us four brothers had planned a trip with our father to Northern Saskatchewan to a fishing resort for fun, relaxation and quality time as a family and fish.

Dad was so excited about the trip. All the brothers got together and purchased Dad is some favourite fishing gear just for this special occasion with our father and his boys. Days leading up to the trip and his murder he would come over to my house, gather all his fishing gear on the back deck and continually clean, polish, sort and arrange everything in his gear making sure everything was exactly right. I had not seen dad wear a smile as big as he had and actual tears in his eyes and him saying to us "THIS IS SUCH A WONDERFUL THING YOU BOYS HAVE DONE" my God we were all so happy and a saying it is a wonderful thing seeing him this way so happy. We were all looking forward to the trip!!

The trip never happened, and that memory will live forever with us brothers as a week before the trip dad was murdered June 1, 2002, Saturday morning. Another day that will live in our memories and tore at all the Stanley family was the day we laid our loving father to rest in his grave. The same day of the funeral, the brothers and families and our father were to travel on our fishing trip. One year later Byron, Wayne, Rick, and I along with other members of the family took the fishing trip in dads' memory and had dads fishing gear with us and to top the fishing trip dads fishing gear caught the first fish. Dad was with us on the trip for sure. We all love you and miss you.

THE CONFERENCE

(The meeting)

> **A Criminal Act can take countless forms, as can Justice and Healing. This conference takes account of the harm, the harmed, Justice and Healing within Restorative Justice picture.**

Finally, a young man stricken with guilt came forward and confessed. The police did say the teen was under the radar when one of the persons in the group found out the first person the police had was not the one responsible for the murder. With this information and questions were asked by the investigators. This person could not answer the questions and could not fill in the blanks the police had. Because of the information and evidence discovered, the person that came forward was released but stayed in the radar, if within a year the evidence the police had included this person, he could be arrested and charged in the case of dad's murder.

The family asked if we had a chance to confront the teen that came in and confessed and to see him face to face. That was denied by the detectives for a couple reasons, 1. He was a young offender at the time of the murder, and we would see him in the court. 2. The detectives wanted to protect the teen from the family.

In a turn of events, the youth, and his defence lawyer Rick Stroppel both asked for a meeting with the family. The prosecutor office agreed to the meeting but there would be conditions attached regarding the meeting. One condition was there will be an organization oversee the meeting.

It was agreed by the Prosecutors office, the defense lawyer, and the judge that the Edmonton Restorative Justice Network (ERJN) and Alberta Conflict Transformation Society (ACTS) would oversee the meeting and script a series of questions, recording the responses to each question from every person on both sides (defense family members and the family members on the prosecutors' side).

Other conditions agreed upon was the teen had to commit in pleading guilty to the murder of our father (Robert Stanley) and write a remorseful apology to the Stanley family, letting him explain the situation of himself in the planning and the execution of the murder. At first the arrangement had to be made with the Stanley family and if all the family members did not guarantee the meeting the meeting would not take place. I remember the discussion between the family members and the detectives was very lengthy and at times was emotional with a lot of question asked to clarify the meeting.

Sue Hopgood from ACTS contacted the family and myself and asked if she could meet with me and our the family members to discuss the process of the meeting. She said that the teen and his lawyer was asking for a meeting with the family over the murder of our father. At first our response was a flat "NO WAY." Sue was very persistent on the meeting saying the meeting would be good and that through this encounter could and would fill in any blanks on the case the family had. It took awhile for us to say we would meet with the person that admitted dropping the boulder over the railing onto our father's bus.

It was agreed, my brother Byron and myself would meet with Sue in her office where we were introduced to the Alberta Conflict Transformation Society (ACTS) organization and the conferencing model which would be involved. Sue explained everything in detail. We had countless questions – How would the meeting with the murderer be Good? -How will the meeting help the Family? – What would be the restoration in all our lives? We had lots of other questions asked over the couple of hours we had with Sue.

During the meeting we kept saying, this kid murdered our father, "we should do onto him as he did onto our father." Yes, we frustrated and incredibly angry at the kid. How could this meeting even be thought of? How can we meet with the person that murdered our father in a stupid senseless act? Remorseful, how could this kid be remorseful – he committed the premeditated murder and wants to apologize! We said to Sue all this kid wants is a lighter sentence was the thoughts and the family would think and say no dame way, he can burn for what he did.

Again, Sue was patient where she explained what the conference model is about and what it is designed to accomplish. Also, she said if we get to the meeting and for any reason or at anytime, we could get up and walk out. Sue explained that the conference was a scripted process where the same questions were asked to everyone in the conference. Everyone has a chance to ask question of their own to the offender also speak in their own words on their feelings. In turn the offender has a chance to speak to the family.

Over the weeks from June 4, 2006, four years after the death of our father, and the discussion with the family about the conference we agreed to pursue Resolution through ACTS and ERJN and to try community conferencing, not everyone was at the meeting. Some could not make it, or others did not want to be part of it and did not like what was happening. Everyone has their opinions. But we as a family wanted to find out where this kids mind was just to think of doing such an outrageous thing. Dropping a 30-pound boulder, pushing it through the holes cut out of the steel meshing by the persons onto a vehicle traveling at high speed, hoping to do what. The act was as they thought was fun at the time only to scare or damage a vehicle but ended the life of Robert Stanley and change the lives forever of the Stanley family.

It came down to a long, hard, and emotional draining conference for twenty-seven family members of both sides lasting an agonizing seven hours in a school gym in the center of Edmonton where the day was extremely hot, and the place did not have air conditioning. Throughout the entire conference there was a large picture (four-foot-wide) of our father with his pipe standing against the school bus he drove. The hole time and the reason the picture stood behind the family is for the offender that murdered our father, when the offender was talking or one of the Stanley family members were talking or asking the questions, he would see, not the person talking but the picture of dad starring at him reminding of the hurt he caused the family.

Throughout the conference every member had the chance to ask of the offender. Question as; Why? – What were you thinking? – Why should we help you? – You cannot help the Stanley family. With these questions and many more questions and after seven long, hot, and emotional hours we as a family witnessed the true meaning of remorse. True remorse not by definition but see the offender look at who ever was talking, see the eyes as he was listening, see the color and inside the eyes of the person, where the non remorse action would be dark eyes and not looking at the one speaking to him and staring at the floor. This was answered through the entire conference by the offender never took his eyes off the person that was talking. It was evident with tears from the offender, weakness in sitting in the chair and he even passed out from the emotion. Also, the conference had to be stopped a couple of times for the offender had an extreme challenging time and the detective and the mediator had to take him into the hallway making sure he was fit to continue.

As was said earlier the difference in a person lying and the person telling the truth and the sincerity as is the liar has a blank look and the eyes seem to black with no depth where on the other hand a person telling the truth and sincerity the eye are different.

They will have color and the staring is a look with a sole that can be seen. The other indicator is the body language, sitting up not slouching, sitting with the interested posture look like part of the conversation and the emotion state being real. Throughout the meeting the words and actions are true remorse which the family when met aside after at the conclusion and discussing seen it and agreed the offender had remorse in doing the act and taking our father from us. To witness this is more than the meaning of remorse not just the definition. I recall the family including myself had normal thoughts of anger and revenge "but it was through the feelings and seeing the emotions and actions of the offender's remorse that change me and effected my life.

Some of the family had trouble looking at this young person and the actions he committed in the murder of our father and thinking how we as individuals and family could forgive him. That was the hardest thought in the minds of the family and thinking "how could we forgive this person." Knowing what he had done in destroying the lives of the family. Yet he was sitting in front of the Stanley family, not asking but demonstrating how sorry he truly was and how this all has affected him wishing this never happened. The remorse was haunted his being. The question is - **WHY?**

The person in front of the family did not look the part of a criminal. He looked to innocent, weak and vulnerable. We all asked each other how could this person be a criminal? During our breaks in the conference, we as a family gathered and reflected the process of the meeting and what we just witnessed and heard. We did not look at this person as a nineteen-year-old but as a fifteen-year-old boy who was good looking, great grades in school and never been in trouble with the law. You could tell he was just a young kid even after four years who lost connection with reality for a moment in time. He Also had a broken family where the support and the help were not evident. Most of his members of the family had not much to say in the conference, which seemed different from our family's interest in the conference circle. His family had an "oh hum attitude" and by watching the body languages of each member of his family except for one person they were not a supporting family.

Dads' memory came at us like we never new before. We asked ourselves, does this young boy deserve a chance to better himself or do we walk away and let the system deal with him. As a family we all thought of our father (it was if he was in the room with us). How would dad deal with this? In his love, harshness and rough character but being the gentle giant, he would give you another chance with a lot talking on the good and the bad. His fairness in dealing with discipline was what came to all his sons (Byron, Rick, Wayne, and myself).

So as a family we talked together for what it was an exceptionally long time, we asked ourselves. – Can this person be saved? – Does he deserve a break from the family? - Can we forgive him for the actions he did in the murder of our father? If the answer is 'yes,' then you as the offender must reform and lead a positive life. We as a family, on the wishes of our father, have always been saying, "we will have no part in creating a lifetime criminal." We also discussed the young boy, in front of us may not survive incarceration either.

We asked what the other avenues are there was for us to consider. We were told that through the impact statements the voice of the family would be heard loudly as a group in asking of no to incarceration but restoring the life of this young boy. At the end of the conference, one thing is the family forgave the actions only if he complied to all the courts demands, moved on to a new life and never forget the break he received from family devastated with the sudden loss of the beloved father, grandfather, and husband (Giving his life a chance). The only thing that will live on for the rest of our lives is the that our father was murdered through the actions of an inconsiderate young offender, not realizing consequences of unfolded through this prank that went wrong for the young man.

"THE FOOTPRINTS IN THE SAND"

I do not understand why, when I
need you most. You leave me.
He whispered.
My precious child, I love you and
will never leave you, never,
ever during the trials and testing's
When you only see one set of FOOTPRINTS
It was then I carried you.

THE STANLEY FAMILY MAKES
THE RIGHT CHOICE

Today I am saying "we made the right decision." We stayed in touch all the time, making certain he was complying, and we are now he himself made the choice to follow his dream in improving and living life to the best and moved on the proper way, completing his studies in university. He moved on to become a productive member of society. The words I said to him at the conference was holding and squeezing his hand not in a hand shack "in any way you break the agreement of the courts and Stanley family's or turn back to crime you are standing from of the very angry person that will drag your ass to jail personally." He has become a model citizen moved on. I am thankful and speak for the family "the right choice was made"

As the title reads, we gave the offender a chance to continue his life and go on and do the right thing for society and especially the Stanley family, his family and himself. Our family after the conference saw inside of him and witnessed a young person wanting a chance and asking forgiveness. It will be and was hard to think of forgiveness as he took someone away from the family. So, we all concluded we would never forget but under condition we could forgive him in a way we understood this person was young and what we had seen in the meeting truly little support from a fragmented family. As we all said in the conference to him, we see good now in you so do not disappoint and of the people from our side and your side and especially yourself. To this day asking how the offender we met in the worst part of our lives was doing. I personally do not contact him; I go through the RJ Society saying he is doing good.

TURNING POINT

The old ways of doing things does not work, if you want real chance, communication, and education in themselves are preventative activities. It is about putting our energy in the right place, with parents, schools, and teachers and with communities. An eye for an eye is barbaric, it does not work. The ways of the old west are gone.

COMMUNICATION – by understanding your fellow being, listening to the ones that cry for a chance to change and want to mold themselves into today's society. The future within the Justice System I believe is looking for an alternative way for Society to mold the golden ones, the children of the future.

EDUCATION – a systematic process through which a child or an adult acquires knowledge, experience, skill, and sound attitude. Making individuals civilized, refined, cultured, and educated.

Do not be fooled with the career criminal. They are not there for the good of society and will if given a chance to fool people, those individuals just want to be free, will fool the system into a chance to out into the public, eventually reoffend. The Restorative Justice communities would be able to weed these types out. Restorative Justice is not meant to replace the court system but to through mediation between the person(s) that are harmed and the person(s) doing the harm. Through this process, remorse would be shown through the actions and body positions. The true remorseful criminals would be the same as in my experience in my father murder case. Understanding remorse, one must witness it for themselves. Remorse is seeing within the eyes and not looking into dark lifeless eyes that have life and color also with their body language during the interview.

The system would collaborate with communities and enforcement agencies to help find candidates that Restorative Justice will work for those individuals chosen. How even today most criminals have already been molded for society. The innocent ones would be the toughest to find. Ones found, conferencing will be the tools mentioned like communication, education and understanding. Listening to the troubled person is sometimes the only tool that is needed to turn a person.

Sometimes it is an apology, can be financial and in cases an agreement between the harmed and harmer is made and mentoring on others. There is far more freedom and thought in schools than in the Criminal Justice System, but the goal is always to stop troubled person(s) exhibiting emotional or behaviour problems.

Sue Hopgood (my mentor) has said studies indicate policies are not being overused but are also counter productive and ineffective. As in industrial application – layoff – suspension is the negative solution were working the persons emotions and/or behavior towards others into a positive solution in the harm.

Working with the harmed and the harmer will help physically and emotionally in solving a common latitude where the repair can be worked out. So negative attitudes can and will produce greater harm to the person(s) instead of looking for punishment the two (harmed and harmer) can come to a resolution that they can agree to and feel good about it.

<u>RESTORATIVE JUSTICE WILL AND DOES WORK</u>

— SUN photos by PERRY MAH

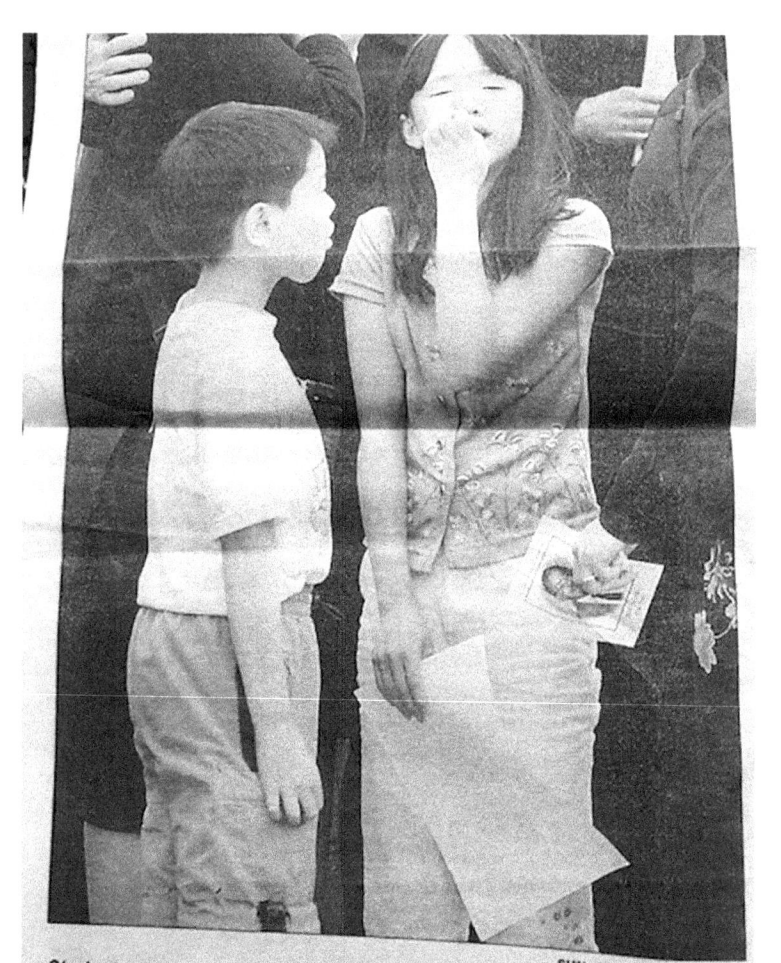

Students, teachers and parents from Our Lady of the Prairies Catholic school are grief-stricken after the funeral service for bus driver Bob Stanley at West Edmonton Christian Assembly yesterday.

CHAPTER IV

RESTORATIVE JUSTICE DIRECTION

My life has changed in the way I look at Justice in my everyday life.

"Forgiveness is a strong attribute"

I am now actively dedicating my energy to creating positive change in the Canadian Justice System. Witnessing the personal, experience and experiencing accountability seeing sincere remorse from an offender changed me from a pay back attitude and reprisal to a state of pride. I feel pride in how the family managed the conferencing session the results and in a young man change. I am proud of who I am and what I am doing. I thank my father and brothers for leading me to a life with the same values and integrity that our father lived with.

My association with Sue Hopgood formed during the community conference. Sue oversaw as the director of the Alberta Conflict Transformation Society (ACTS) during the murder of my father. With the participation in the conference, Sue asked me to join the (ACTS) board of the new system in Restorative Justice. At first, I asked how I can be part it. I am not a lawyer, police officer, a prosecutor, a defense lawyer, but in the meetings, they said I fit perfect. My response was 'Yah Sure." Then Sue said to me, I have the one thing none of rest have, the experience of being part of conferencing in my fathers' murder and bring to the table the power of message. I did accept the honour of the invitation and joined Acts as a board member. I served on the board for five years involved in developing and part of information to program development. In interviewing Sue, journalist writer Jamie Hill,

Sue talked about me I the Society and described me and quoted her "he is like French Beard – crusty on the outside but soft on the inside." I did like the comparison.

Throughout the time on the board, I was speaking to diverse groups and organizations also as a guest speaker Conferencing Training and a participant guest speaker at Restorative Justice Conferences such as in Banff, at colleges especially with my father's murder and the conference the participated in. Through speaking and training in Conferences, in decided the way I view harm changes how I thought of Alternative solution instead of thinking like a hard ball. This affected me in my job as a safety professional. Instead of viewing the facts and not listening to the people that committed the harm, I shifted into the most powerful way, and that is, becoming a great listener. Through listening I had time to hear the person(s) talk and giving me a better way to resolve the harm committed.

As written in the first part, Restorative Justice encompasses these five elements:

1. <u>Meeting</u> – between the person(s) who are harmed and the person(s) committing the harm. Where the victim and the offender volunteer to meet.
2. <u>Narrative</u> – This is where a set of questions are developed and where each of the sides listen to the answers with no interruptions and each having their turn to respond.
3. <u>The Emotional</u> – Traumatized victims show their harm committed to the person(s) and demonstrates emotions talking how it affects their lives. At this

point is where the remorse could be evident from the person(s) that committed the harm.
4. <u>Understanding the process</u> – Crime causes harm and justice requires repairing that harm. Through conferencing, the process is developed to begin the repair and understanding in listening power.
5. <u>Agreement</u> – AT this point the harm is resolved. Where the person(s) harmed and the person(s) committing the hard agree on a fair outcome. Resolution may not be agreed; however, the case has been heard between the person(s) affected. A fair outcome may also be delayed which could be for or against the meeting. In the end the case has gone through the process.

Restorative Justice can be used to reduce the burden in the criminal justice system, to divert cause out of the system and to provide the system with a range of constructive sanctions. Law and traditional justice practices have led to calls for an alternative response to crime and social disorder. These alternatives provide the parties involved, and often communities, the opportunity to participate in resolving conflict and addressing consequences. Restorative Justice are based on the belief that parties to a conflict must be actively involved in the resolution and mitigation its negative consequences.

The Restorative outcome is finalized in an agreement reached because of the process. The agreement may include referrals to the programme such as – make amends for the wrong committed against the person(s) or community, restitution and community services which is aimed to meeting the individual and collective needs and responsibilities of the parties and achieving the restoration of the victim and the offender. Other measures may be combined in cases involving serious offenses.

The conferencing the family went through that day was long, hot, and changed the demeaner of the Stanley family. This was an impressive act on everyone coming from "an eye for an eye" to relaxed siding with a lessor attitude towards the offender sitting in front of us. We as a family now new the process in Restorative Justice and how it was meant to work.

This was demonstrated when the first offender stood, turned to the family, the offender reliving the horrific day where he took the life of our father, looking at each member of my family in true remorse spoke to each of us. With the second offender was different from the first offender. That offender did not show the remorse as the first one did only by staring at the floor where the first one looked at each of us in the court room and the second offender only word said was sorry. No remorse was evident at that moment in court. The second offender with no feeling for his participation in the murder, tears and looked like he did not want to say a word.

FORGIVE AND FORGET

Again, there is a definition describing the words remorse, but that is far from the visual effect as I witnessed for myself. How an individual feels inside (heart ache, turning stomach, nervousness, sweaty, blurred thoughts, and the vision of the harm committed). In the murder case of our father. To forgive and forget is extremely hard to commit to.

As in the case of our father, not everyone could come to grips with forgiveness, and forgetting is something that stays in the memory forever. I summed it up when asked, as the harm is burned into our memories, that harm can not be erased. As for the forgiveness, the way I consider this point is, a person can forgive the actions leading to the harm, as people can forgive. It is in our growing up that we all have committed harm in the past. Therefore, I do forgive the actions because of the lack of guidance in the youth years, the teaching of right from wrong and the pier pressure in the younger years.

GIVE LIFE A CHANCE

As forgiveness is often defined as an individual, voluntary internal process of letting go of the feelings and thoughts of resentment, bitterness, anger and the need for vengeance and retribution towards someone who believe has wronged us, including ourselves. Both forgiveness and revenge are social instincts, these are fixed aspects of human nature, these capabilities can be altered which gives us hope that we can make the world a more forgiving and less vengeful place. (McCullough, 2008)

Research in positive psychology and elsewhere shows the outcomes of forgiveness that have been found to have an impact on overall wellbeing include:

- Reduction of negative affect and depressive symptoms
- Restorative of positive thinking
- Restoration of relationships
- Reduction in anxiety
- Strengthened spirituality
- Raise self-esteem
- A great sense of hope greater capability for conflict management and
- Greater ability to cope with stress and find relief

With forgetting a serious harm committed to people, people do forget. How they forget is a failure in memory retrieval. Your memory of an event, where the keys are, or forgetting the procedure, the memories are still stored in the brain.

These forgotten memories can be brought back intime or when a related subject helps the memory to return. When a serious harm as murder of a loved one happens, the memory is also stored but it will be brought forward easier when the person is reminded through actions and person close to you or an event to name a few.

As in our fathers' case, I have the strongest vision and memory the day he was murdered. I was standing at the front door waiting for my father to pick me up, while watching the news and seeing the picture of the bus on the freeway. There was also the phone call from the police as I was watching the news that my father was seriously injured in an accident. Those first serious of events in the memories of my life with my father and the family will be recalled to me whether sitting looking at pictures or where we at anytime of my life up to the incident. Even though the incident is in my memory, it is not forgotten but put away until a related event happens which at that point the memory if recalled.

In the end, I have forgiven the person but not the action but will never forget how, when and who committed the murder. I have moved on with my life where the Restorative Justice training and practice has helped me. I am following the process and hope to continue my education in Restorative Justice.

I would like to acknowledge Susan Hopgood (introducing me to Restorative Justice and mentoring me) Caroline Gosling (introducing me to Restorative Justice and mentoring me)

Howard Zehr the founder, educator and writer in Restorative Justice, Dave Gustafson for the materials in the study and of course I could not have completed this book without the support of Restorative Justice Society and Community in keeping me in the loop.

ROBERT BRUCE STANLEY BIO

I am the eldest son of Robert (Bob) and Audrey Stanley, Born in Medicine Hat, Alberta June 16, 1949.

Throughout my younger life I had the opportunity to travel and lived in Europe also throughout Canada from Ottawa to Vancouver Island. This was made possible by my father being in the Canadian Air Force stationed at location throughout Europe and Canada.

My family loved life, was a loving and remarkably close knit. This made us all proud and who was responsible, our father and mother. They went out of their way to make sure their children had the best gifts they could give and of course an excellent quality for life.

My father had the gift that every person would ever want, caring, friendship, helping hand and most all the biggest one happy guy. All these traits were passed to all his sons and to this day I can honestly say with pride, me and my brothers have not a mean streak in us.

Throughout my life, I explored different paths,

- A job as a farmer in1967 (that did not fit me at all)
- Surveying 1967-1969 (it was good but as a young guy I needed more excitement)
- The Army, 3rd PPCLI (Princess Patricia's Canadian Light Infantry) which I joined 1972 (it was not for me)

- Then into the Transportation Industry, began in Vancouver and Victoria as a bus driver in 1975
- Transportation has been in me since, right up to the present

From there I moved around and ended in Edmonton in 1980 where I was joined by my mother, Father, and brothers, who followed me. I pursued the transportation industry in safety, trucking, and tour bus throughout Western Canada I am still working.

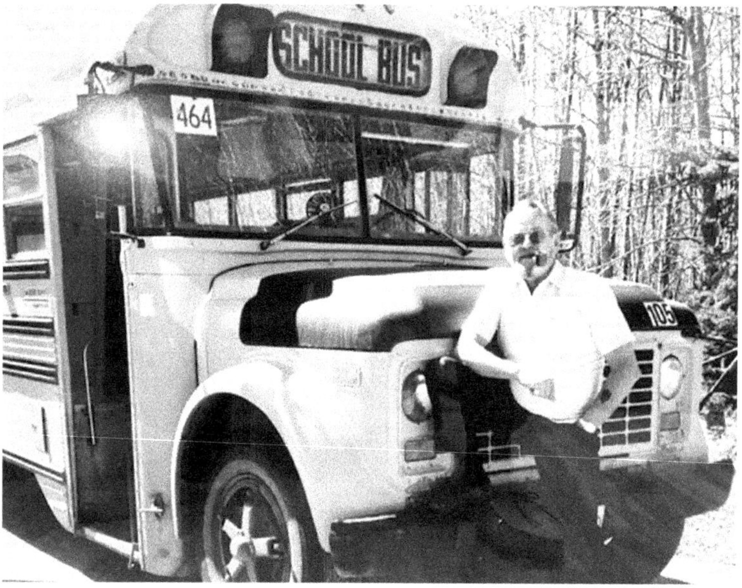
SCHOOL BUS
464
105

CPSIA information can be obtained
at www.ICGtesting.com
Printed in the USA
LVHW010723071222
734662LV00008B/392